Two Bison Confer on Past and Future Wanderings

KEITH MOUL

Acknowledgments

Aji: Fish Scales

Alliterati: Baseball

Ann Arbor Review: Milton Friedman Revels; Venom, Virtue and Fun

Blazevox: Lines

Burning Word: Rebellion Takes up Conspiracy with Mankind

Cirque: Ball Scores Move on

Colere: Drops of Water in the World; Worlds in a Drop of Water

College Poetry Review: Adam

Door Is a Jar: Five in a Day at the Bay: Pathetic Fallacy; Possible Parallels; Thoroughbreds Race, an Allegorical Polemic

Duane's New Poe Tree: Resistance

Greensilk Journal: Photo Dreams at Thanksgiving

Hamilton Stone Review: Malice; Star Matter at Work

Hedge Apple: Spring Tumbles Anew from Slush; Unwelcome with My Camera

Litbreak: Options

Nthanda Review: Come on Fairy; No Words

Midlands: The Volute of Athena's Pillar

Militant Thistles (The Recusant): Ode to Mitch

October Hill Magazine: Patience and Urgency

Pangolin Review: Ideas Relegated; Missed Opportunity over Coffee

Panoplyzine: Walking Stick, a Prayer

Pennsylvania Literary Journal: Ascent without a Firm Link; Curious Oddities; In Dubrovnik

Pif Magazine: Diplomacy's Obligation to History

Porridge: Misty Circumlocution

Rabid Oak: Nearby, but Incognito

Reality Beach: A Place Interstitial; Government Man; Illahee: The Mukilteo to Clinton Ferry

Red Wheelbarrow: A Chip on my Shoulder

Scarlet Leaf Review: Expected Disappearance; Go Somewhere without Saying; Prerogatives

Suisun Valley Review: Tending Roses, an Observance

The Literary Yard: In Memory of Ken Patterson; Opportunity; The Cratered Road to Malancourt;Today at the Pier; Tourists' Pleasure

The Montuckey Review: Impending Weather

The Path: Early Workday at the Marina

The Raven Review: Ever Improving

The Recusant: Olympic Discovery Trail Monday Questions (which includes Forest Disciple Stripped; Midwesterner as Tourist; The Beak Penetrates); Reconstruction, a Conversation

The Sewanee Review: The Seafarer

The Wayfarer: Rust Honors a Bloom; Shorebirds off the Salish Sea

The Write Room: Drama beneath an Alder; Refuge

The Writing Disorder: Thudding Night Rain

Third Wednesday: One Cat of Many; Pride of Lions

Vending Machine Press: Voices in the Belfry

Vision with Voices: Doubloon; Reading at Park Place Books; St. Croix, a Time Ago

Western Humanities Review: Aerial Poems: The Coming of the Circus; Siccitas

Westward Quarterly: I Pause at the Lake to Wait for You

Contents

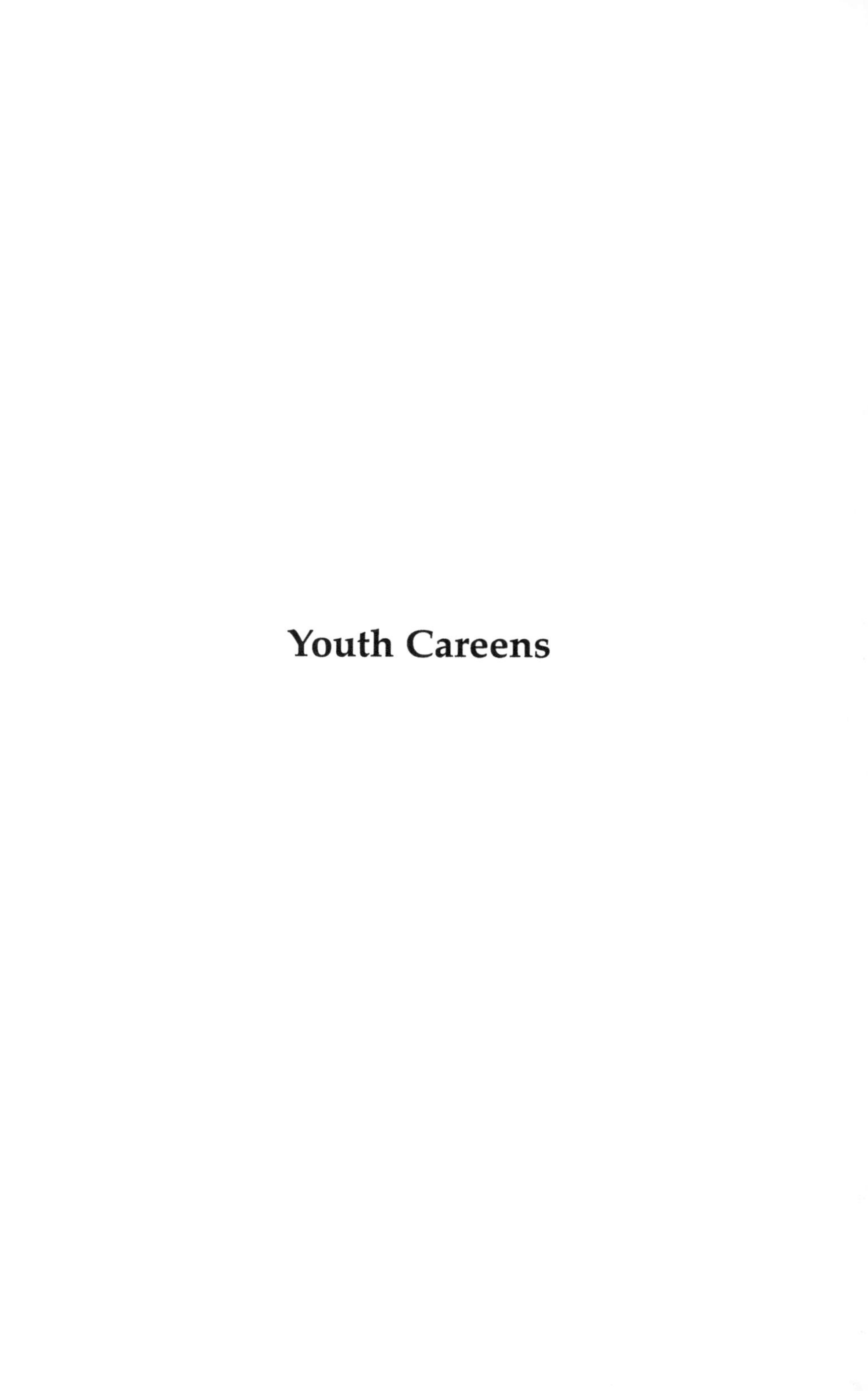

Youth Careens

1944 Privately Remembered

To do his duty at sea, to hear torpedo wakes bubble
up at him from unknowable depths, her man ships
off to serve a new sonar-submerged world.

Echo beeps eerily persist at the edge of sleep,

He rests on deck. Her soul licks the fine hairs
on his ear and whispers "Do you remember?"

More sounds well up from a dark unconscious.

(Back another dip into memory) fighter engines
belch exhaust to start, sounding like emphysema
at the final stage, as remembered in the family.

An Unmarred Tabula
Revisiting my past

Eero Saarinen's Arch
ascended as uncritical assent to lies cited
so often as to become an epitome of dream.
It gleamed a stainless steel halo over St. Louis
as though blessed to stand for a river's life,
to light the gateway to treasure so immense
it needed a Mississippi watershed to lave it.
Add iron horses gliding toward a sure purpose,
perhaps a politics not before, or since, achieved.

When 20, I was no competent witness: I had no
vision, no poetry, not even theory: the legs rose
from piles rammed as if deranged on center earth;
I imagine ringing thunder now; I circled the city
for any vantage, but no view rose to turn my head.

But way above in air Eero saw a predestined atom,
infinitesimal source of the grand augur of the birth:
each minute to month extolling a brilliant testimony.
Deliberately the arch rose up to 606 feet to welcome
that same atom, never stilled, or so it seems, two ends
timed to engage like spacecraft docking in the station.

We all know that science can fill a national purpose,
but a reflective oddity of art is applauded differently.

At 75, my bones, brittled with weight of myth, are free
to hold empty destiny that would be manifest; empire
in which so many of us had no place; a perverse copy
of Locke's *utopia*, I argue should be the commonwealth.

The Volute of Athena's Pillar

In her scroll the marbled future can be read,
while I see her in low relief, crying;
I can hear her torment; she is dying;
beneath the weight of Hymettus, she is dead.

Presence taunts obscurely, yet is a lie:
it is not now what is, or what should be,
that lingers, seldom fervently, with me.
Sense is all I have and time but a sigh.

I spiral through an unresponsive mass
for which most must live, dying alone;
an emptiness that never could atone
for loneliness; to gratify, all pass.

Adam

As all is new, time, of course, is the issue.
How long in the cycle was Eden existent?
Was every chrysanthemum in place, those
peculiar spiky trees, all the surrounds too?

Frankly, it looked a bit scruffy when I woke,
not that I was experienced, no diorama, no
papyrus scrolls, not even music piped in.

But it has been warm, ripe fruit, saturated
colors, particularly the greens and yellows.
And all this before I started breathing. Whew!

Strange to think it sensual as I conceive it,
for outside time the world is lacking process
and I think I impart its motion with my birth.

Wait! Here are instructions: wait in silence;
think about my own blank mind (what?),
soon to be the master die of my impressions.

747

You won the waste sky, bird,
gained an enthused following
for 50 and gaining years.

Your wings glistened from
your fat cabin too gross itself;
you gorged yourself on wide-eyed
morsels lounging softly, foamed
within your steel. Such is glamor,
big bird, to chew the insect
bewildered by alluring lines
and symmetry routing flight.

You fall at times into the sea
but not outside statistical norms.

Older Youth Careens More

The Seafarer

I speak of sufferings   that I have stood to,
hardships to rock   the heart. The times
of breast-cares stretch   from breaking days
toward a bitter dark,   as down the sea-track
I steer by stars   a strange, sad ship.
The dread waves crash,   ever dog my keel
through narrow nightwatch   as I, knitted to stiff oars,
keep her off the cliffs.   Cold clamps my feet
in silence, unseen   steals my limbs
with numbing grip;   while griefs yet quicken
hotly through the heart   and hunger within tears at
the sea-wearied spirit.
                              What spasm of thought
wakes any man   who walks this world
to know the wretchedness   I dwell in, know
the ice-cold sea   I wander, its swept track
alien to my kind?
    Where ice hangs in air   and hail knocks against the storm
I hear only wave-roar   wasted on the sea,
the sounding cold.   At times the swan's song
does me for a joy,   a desperate gaiety;
but the gannet's, curlew's cry   gags the crow of men;
and gulls mark a wide sea   with no memory of mead.
Terns there restate the storm's   beating the stony cliffs,
terns with icy feathers   where eagles turn, on like shrieks,
around and around—   the raging spirit
feels no solace   when a kinsman's face is desolate.
    Indeed he owns nothing of pain   who, proud and merry with
wine,

rioting through the towns,   takes life's pleasures;
nor truly will he ever trust   my telling of the wretchedness,
how, weary to rage,   yet must I wander, and wait.
     Night's shade deepened,   from the north it snowed,
frost gripped the earth,   hail too fell
the coldest of kernels.   Yes, crowding thoughts
leapt the spirit   that I sought the sea's depth,
the salt-wave's motion   to move singly on—
and now every longing   urges me onward
to war against the waters,   wandering hence
to distant lands,   alien and strange.
     Yet no worldly man   weens a mind so lofty,
his gifts so good   nor his deeds that gallant,
nor a frame so mightily thewed,   master so friendly
to never fear   his faring on the sea,
or what the Lord holds,   waiting in the dark hall.
Here is no harping,   no hoard to be dispensed,
no pleasure in a woman—   nowhere a worldly joy!—
nothing, nothing, nothing   but the night-black waves.
Who sets out eagerly   ever longs with the sea.
     Flowers fill the groves;   faces of towns,
meadows brighten   and the world stirs busily:
everything spurs   the eager heart,
that beating to put bow   to a breaking sea
when spirit swells   to hoist up sail again;
even as the cuckoo   calls out sorrowfully,
the ward of summer   singing only sadness,
the bitter feelings of his breast.   He blessed with comfort
can not know, only dreads   this destiny we bear,
we who tread alone   the farthest tracks of exile.
     And yet, now, my heart would burst   the limits of my breast,
my spirit resound   the rhythms of the sea,
hunt widely the whale,   its isolated haunts

throughout the cold expanse,   and then come back to me,
eager, and with greed: one gull screams,
rouses to the whale's way   the heart, irresistibly
however broad the wake.   Warmer for me
those lordly joys   than this dead life
fleeing, too, this land.
                              I do not believe
the wealth of earth   stands, for them, unendingly.
For, to each, his final hour   fetches doubt of things,
which of three his fate   shall finally be:
sickness, old age,   the sword of hate?
All wager   none will be withstood!
So, let praise live   best in lasting words
for every earl   by those speaking after;
let that be earned   before his eyes forever close,
by holding stead,   conquering hatred;
building deeds   boldly against a devil,
that men's sons extol him   ever after.
May his self live on,   as an angelic song
strikes the ear,   eternally,
a gladness to the host.
                              For the glitter is gone,
kingdoms stand, emptied   of earth's spectacle,
and kings dead, emperors   darkened like the day.
No gold is proffered   and the gold-givers gone
whose glory shown   in the greatness of their deeds;
gone all who lived   in lordliest luster.
Fallen the noble warriors,   the frail joys fallen
to weaker hearts   who mark this world
by fruitless toil.   Fame perishes,
the noble order   ages, fades
to now like any man   married to the earth:
with palsied body,   face grown pale,

the white-haired one weeps,   aware that his old friend,
the line of princes,   alters with the loam.
    The body, lifeless,   barren of its senses,
savors no sweetness,   nor the sear of pain,
nor the hand's motion,   nor the mind's myth.
Though a brother strew   a brother's grave
with glorious treasures,   gold from hoards
that kept him through this life,   to keep him in the next,
the body will turn   to death's touch
and the black soul   flee the body,
leave it to its emptiness   and the terror of the earth.

Aerial Poems: Coming of the Circus

A hot coming we had of it,
just the worst time of the year
for a circus, after a long journey:
bleary roads and the corn head high,
the lion whelps still training.
and the pick-up stalled, paint peeling, transmission bad,
leaking oil in the prairie dust.
There were times we regretted
Harry's split with P.T. Barnum, the ready crowds
and the big-town girls, unescorted.
Then the camel men cursing and grumbling
and running away, departing for Yemen on Thursday,
performances on Saturday, each taking his camel,
with citizens crazy for one-humped ruminants,
and July limp as a flower in the Iowa sun:
no cool time we had of it.
Towards the end we harried and practiced all night,
sleeping in hammocks,
with the voices blaring in dull ears, saying
that all this was folly.

Saturday they came with their quarters and dollar bills,
wet with their morning sweat, smelling of vegetation;
faded overalls and white paper fans beating the thick air,
suspicion cooling big eyes,
enough to freeze even the cream of aerial acts.

Then, the old tent falsetto, filled with the egregious host,
six hands at the entrance, all tearing in two of the tickets,

and feet stomping the planks of rough pine.
Harry, red in the big, white light, hailed now for attention
with arresting power, not a moment too soon
quelling the place; it was (you may say) another beginning.

All this was a long time ago, I remember,
and I would do it again, but think now
think on this
think: did we come all that way for
eminence, ease? There was no ease, certainly,
we had evidence and no doubt. I had seen comfort and fame,
and was sure they were different; our fame was
shock, and the empty dust of us, failure, infame.
We adjourned to the hostel, bright neon,
but no longer at ease there, in the old dispensation,
with the lingering stink and waul of the Big Top.
There could be wealth in another town.

Aerial Poems: SICCITAS*

¿Por que aqui?   ¿A Iowa?   ¿Quien Sabe?

What dearth what signs what wonders and what sand waves
abrasing our desert ship
the scent of grass of the prairie soaring through the air
what images returned
O who knows why.

Those who frequent the tent of our dust, meaning
Them
those whose ice eyes glitter from the warped bows
    of the green planks, meaning
Them
those who sit in the sty of contentment, meaning
Them
those who inspire the rank odor of the animals, meaning
Them

Are become our whole substance blown in by the wind,
eructation, of the prairie wind
to this place absurd in this place

Why in this place, unclear but clearly
the pulse of our strength, less strong yet stronger—
profit or not? Remote as Chicago, New York or LA

Whispers and weak laughter between the groans and
    the hurrying feet
under tents, where all the clever meet.

Pack truck cracked of block and paint cracked with heat
Why this place?, it is forgotten
unremembered.
The rigging weak and the canvas rotten
between one June and another September.
eyes of the uncaring, half conscious, open, my own.
Engagement two weeks, each will goggle twice.
Cackle, struggle, wallow.
Desirous of passage to the wide-open sea; let us
ship on the wide wind like a desert ark sails extended
toward the sea, sand parting, the hope, to the sea.

What seas what signs what wonders wondrous what images
of eyelids closing in the dust
of Iowa.

*Latin for drought or dullness (of style)

Primeval Vision of a Gull

Space encircles a gull: it never needs to imagine an endless universe.
This gull has plenty—water trajected to whitecaps; land shaken to hills
that form semblances; constant flow to sculpt beliefs from timeless
rocks—
this gull carves its space to lift white wings, to push at wind its breast,
burns incandescent as if its light were borne here from an original star.

I dream my oracular gull. I ban its usual garbage scavenge with
cockroach
and rat swilling; I ban the fish—I ban too the gull's mindless stare:
its eye
of original genius slows time; it witnesses gods setting a meal of
ambrosia.

Having understood, I am tail to its driving wings, exploration's
rudder over
green peninsulas, through cutting straits, so much of my special
imaginings
to allow access like clouds, the gull as my mount, at its reins I
release control
to accompany an animal, free of hunger, setting its course beyond
the gates.

Baseball

Many of us like the games. I admire the workings:
seasons spring to fall disfigure fields and, so, the crew
must do its work or the umpire must call "unplayable";
delays under lights; bees or June bugs seeking eyes
and ears; youngsters bonked by liners in opposite stands,
foul balls; peanut, beer and popcorn vendors, games
at their backs, ones, fives, tens and twenties finger-close
at their fronts heralding last call, even with extra innings.

Summer outs scar the innings, yet grease the workings,
totaling runs, hits and errors until the winning is done,
winners' joys caught in the throat of winning's thrill.

Gamble on the tally, if you must, but load the weight
with the pitcher's grinding will: a man on third with
less than two away, in the eighth, or in the ninth, numbers
exploding game-time like flesh in an ever-festering wound;

the dice tumble…and stop, bright ivory, black holes, green envy,
red face, yellow down the back: what's a screaming liner to third,
fierce colliding spikes, blood on leather to the best of winter friends?

St. Croix, a Time Ago

Yes, I remember its eminence:
the restaurant overlooking
a fertile valley, hot and humid,
but paradise for many.

I remember sun burnishing
the early evening, softening
in tropical languor.

You continue to think of the steak.

Lines

Now and as I foresee,
I revere fine, straight lines—
such as those too uncanny
for a map, mind-lines
taking me from here to there,
now to then—
until this instant that I breathe,
this cadence that I walk to,
that is,
because *there* and *then,*
if birds,
would be birds of prey
and ravenous.

What should be simple routes
returning to here and now
are marred by wing beats,
scarred by talons
clicking across them awkwardly.

Sometimes I know
that birds of prey,
hungry for flesh,
will even eat a line
conceived utterly as meat of the mind.

Come on Fairy

(paean to Sylvia)

Human acts buzz as foreign noise to small birds:
animal jurisdiction rests in the trees not the court;
birds zip by, casually native, whoop songs with it;
mean feathered crows from the neighborhood add
cacophony but cannot drive away a laughing man.

No one wants a brown spring: yet flat platitudes,
wrens piping a heavy warmth dour with summer.
Any whiff of cool air circles way up in the south.

I am of two minds about spring: this early without
crocus, wet and delicious, over bright green sprigs;
then later what I wanted all along, voracious revival
of growth dead set on sunlight and extra shares of air.

Aw come on fairy, your earnestness has moved me
into mud, first only one knee, then both at a time,
so my butt inevitably immerses into the icy cold,
swells red and tingling, meets yours in happy slime.

Opportunity

Discerning fully its act, Genius breaks into a glass house,
breaking glass but indifferent to its breaking felony LAW.
Tiny splinters now attend Genius, inhibiting a full search.
More clattering ensues, stark collapse of weakened walls.
Genius understands that walls, windows, or doors may fall
without convulsion of vision through even shards of glass.

Yet Genius must pause, in sharpest peril; it bleeds profusely
as if wounded by events beyond ken, meanings beyond Genius.

It would claim, if caught, this break-in was not premeditated.
Opportunity crimes happen. Genius rehearses without reckoning:
misdemeanor of circumstantial happenstance excused by low funds,
very high testosterone, pouty libido, very much drained, overdrawn.

Genius never frets moral consequences. It neither requires nor gives
advice easily. Genius ignores the thrill of passing parades, coronations;
never respects road signs, storm warnings or evidence of other
GENIUS.

Although this Genius pales toward night, ebbs with loss of puissance,
its tribe of the anointed and marked (to which totems are erected
with many painted faces of beasts) does not relinquish any of its power
with its warrior's decline, or the rise of enemies thought as only
mediocre.

Ball Scores Move on

After ten days in Prague, Budapest,
and Krakow, I miss the April ball scores:

the implications of five to four;
six to one, and eight to nothing;
the 162 game season;
saving the bullpen;
how Baltimore hangs on a chop.

Oh, the designated hitter!
The south paw!

I would love a close play at third,
a cold rain delay of a spring game, even
freezing ropes in the gaps or corners,
where to buy even a scratch hit,
but I don't conjure the old players
or lend my ear to Vin Scully's call.

Separation enlarges into loss; teams
transact with young strangers; owners
learn cold lessons of their ignorant breed.

Heralded retirees quickly reside
in bronze, glimpsed, lovingly rubbed.

Illahee: The Mukilteo to Clinton Ferry

I would not mock headway through the Puget Sound.
Its waters scour painful memories of May last year:
winter white caps bulge with joy indifferent to me;
defy the freeze thermometers insist, by law, and sailors,
by legend, should lock us here in permanent ice pack.

Ilahee's bow conflates that joy with generous space,
roils foam whirlpools and dizzies fish to trail off aft.

Passengers gather, doze or slip into cold air to smoke:
I walk the quivering craft well past her prime, rolling
in her beetle motion beating her time to Whidbey Island.

Too brief a trip to grasp all last spring's parallels: facts
that scarred from their single telling are script enough
to retrace another's happy Sunday trip that ended badly,
theatrically, miscalculated, bloodstained in a drainage ditch.

In Ianthe's scars, my instinct computes faceless contours
of the past, excising obstacles to life at intersecting roads,
pummeling heads of too indifferent drivers turning left
in frequent search to meet some gladly isolated self.

I visit a businessman. He will understand my grief, my
distraction by this tragic serendipity; and he will grasp
that I can not make a lily of a gnarled alder, nor forgive
a negligence, nor in my pain turn a fence post to a rose.

I cannot find the site. Seasons wash away all the blood.
Ice will thaw, its melt obliterate all history, a specter.
Stone-age beetles slug along in ugly court as jesters.

No Words

(Grampa August Uhl 1894-1982)

Morning fills a packing box with doubts. **Gus, vigorous alive;
dead since '82**.

Memories attach to things: documented such as yellow snaps of
the family dead,
(tossed into the box); such as traumatic scribbles on calendar
notes (tossed into the box);
such as letters fleshed from my dreams or fancies (tossed with
contempt into the box);
**such as semi-pro ballplayer; such a story-teller; Gus be-
queathed no written words**.

I pack too what I must not discard: Gus' day-book of 1908:
Cardinals' and Browns'
season of box scores; topped with the Cubs' last world series win
against the Tigers.

My doubts concern my failed duty to him I cherished too late as a
fascinating man.
The trip was only a few miles by car, via I-70. We went every
week, or he and Reg
came to us. My opportunity to measure history was endless. I
goofed off instead.

Alders measure my years here; one dropped in my woods last
night, rotted, consumed

inside, as they will be. **Gus the doughboy sacrificed one eye to Black Jack in 1918.**
Fruitful seasons for peonies, roses and lilies measure Sylvia's years here, and so for me.
Recalcitrant land can be shaped and shifted, drained and pampered at physical cost:
land's scape measures our years here; land's character forces our obeisance no more.

One eye and all, Gus bowled and laughed all night with Reg, girls asleep in the back:
By '82 Gus simply could not make the call: his daughters grabbed his lowered flag:
Clara the bawdy; Marge (Mom) the stoic; Alice with a beer; Ginny, bawdier with 2.

I disdain what I cannot pack: punishing winter winds; a fence forcing deer from their trails;
sinewy blackberry twined with forbidding fruit; dogs whose howls rejoin coyotes' yelps;
eggs of slugs in unimaginable numbers clustered just beneath the cold ground's surface;
slugs in unimaginable numbers, twirling in wet like lotion, striking poses without bones;
slugs feasting on slugs in convulsing slime; slugs captured stone-hard by mid-morning light.

Who knew what steamfitters did, whether during or after the glorious age of steam?

Fortunately those things I cannot pack in easily cannot be abandoned: spring, summer breeze;
deer all around my fence eating tender shoots, doe and fawn

making do, but never a buck;
blackberry jam sweet with tang on English muffin; moving coy-
otes yelp from all directions;
slugs, grand in ascendancy, slugs compelling icons of permanence
among gastropod mollusks.

After Alice died young, the death march began: Reg, Clara, Marge, then the wry Virginia.

Sylvia awoke next to me, pronouncing new considerations of
bright and laughing possessions.
Apparently more packing boxes than expected will be needed.
But in sufficient volume and size.

Gus gave. Reg couldn't get enough, then passed it along in levity
to all the rest of us. **Gus took**
decades of his many lives from me: horseshoes tossed in celebra-
tion; ball played as worship;
beer in pails as neighborly rite most summer nights; ribs crispy
from the backyard fire pit;
patriotic songs as sung by doughboys over there, not by new
jingos pumping breath for war;
to treat kids anywhere as friends; watching fish bubble in the lake;
to fish far from bubbles:
Gus made me a man, accepted fondly my new wife; guided me to fatherhood, seamlessly.

This day I reach, now 68 myself, filling my boxes, my past is me,
my words are our futures.

Misty Circumlocution

Canada geese strut and honk, beaking
spring grass; forsake servility to instinct
to migrate north, then south like tourists
bound to perpetual reservations, the act,
not the attractive vacation destinations.

Maybe they look past the sprouting trees;
wish to think of tree and goose cycles of
life; or consider implications of species;
or stop ceaseless confusion in humid fog.

My own sense of direction can be fallible
during circumlocution in gray winter mist.

Thudding Night Rain
(at my desk)

Finally falls a rain that thuds.
I haven't felt a thud rain for years.
How did I not listen to
and watch the sky for this?

At 1:00 A.M., eagerly, I step outside.

Sod-life relents,
it floats up or burrows down.
Surfaces, melting in dark, shine.
Caught, air assents, helpless.

I open my mouth and ease my parch.
The summer grass sucks noisily;
like air from a pressure vessel,
the ground emits its steam.
I slide barefooted like the boy I am no more.

I have known plentiful bones
bleached by sun,
piled as if by oracles.
What a thudding rain could do
to make believers for life,
refreshed and holy.

But I am alone.
I can only speculate.

I have no link to the heavens

except wet hair,
muddy feet
and torn shirt that binds me.

Housed with their dreams,
do others lie drenched in this awareness?

Fish Scales

(for Ianthe as she completes a painting)

You have come to certainty;
God nor I gave you much help;
some times a fight with order,
time after time vivid colors
flash from you to your canvas.

Then too, when your mind finds
new conceptions, yet alters
course through tangles
of illusion, or swims
from you like a swarm
of fish, darting in silver scales,
sure only within its own numbers,
know we all weigh weaknesses and secrets.

Years ago, in Paris,
I purchased a heavy *History of Art*,
in English, and carried it
from one essential photo to the next,
thinking to sit and enjoy some day,
in mock retirement,
its sweep of forms,
its color contrivances,
its savage, private histories,
the public mysteries of art.

If by any chance, on a morning
you suffer for your art,
your vision will not distill,
fingers fight the brush (wrong brush,
wrong fingers), or a new sun blasts
your canvas until the colors run,
know we all shield our lust
until its discharge points us to our goal.

Younger than Old Keeps on Keeping on

Refuge

A child's natural hatefulness
    always shocks me:
as if teasing a struggling toad
    were a higher joy;
as if letting air out of the soul
    were like letting air out of a ball;
as if other children,
    all other children,
    were private pets
    leashed for new forms of fun.

I have forgotten my cruelties.
I have taken refuge in age.
I have eaten at the hands of kindness.
I have forgiven others for my pain.

Often my mind has been open to trespass;
my child has matured, put aside
most of her childish fears;
our attendance at the feast around us
has quickened the foot
and strengthened the arm.

A child's natural hatefulness
    often saddens me;
as if a large part of me stands by,
    alert but ineffective;
as if my breathing were a selfish act
    that only I hear;

as if the smallest part of me
    turns petty in the face of need,
    demanding my advantages.

A Place Interstitial

A garden slows hurry with hope for
the soil's acolyte, the patron of stars.

As a gardener she ages, more fragile
every day as roots deepen, branches
fill. As her needs increase, I help her
less, in even her rare areas of soft loam.

Two acres have been bountiful source
for vegetables, flowers, and fruit trees:
ten trees gifting us miracle pears, plums,
apples and cherries, but more often not;
scattered herbs, clustered lilies and roses
bunch at horse eye-height. No. No horse.

No miracle of binocular vision, at alert to
see anything, but not spot what I need:
find the blue and yellow sprinkling can?
Luminous, vivid, but for now vanished.

Logs felled at building, now a mute aside,
long ignored for fire or cat funeral bier:
cilia fistulas decay cellulose and moss,
feast on waste. My vision levels there.

I can carry mulch, loyal aide-d-camp, spy
terrain, map a strategy, bury a cat's bones,
rummage through logs for her I love and
trace the unruly tool in flowers among them,

an interstitial place in sometime drought,
needing water, often from a sprinkling can.

I cannot master or possess this garden life,
nor hear its persistent and ennobling call,
but I enlist my back to meet a pressing need
and march a conquerer in triumph, water
brimming a blue and yellow sprinkling can.

Drama Beneath An Alder

I stand beneath the alder tree,
respectfully.
Wind stirs a bit, then more.
The last leaf of its season falls.

Wind bulls in for winter,
grabs my shoulder, twists
me down to the ground.

The new season shivers my soul
but does not shake my respect.

In Dubrovnik

I turn in bed, once again
in touch with my heat. I bear
wakefulness as if a load.

Competing churches toll bells:
half hours at four minute intervals,
ancient rivalries, even wars
over calendars, holy feasts,
even a few commandments.

Light begins a chorus of birds.
excited twitters. Then briefly
silent as humans cough and rush
as for many centuries.

Night has cooled air, not cold,
the surrounding stars
and half moon remain,
not yet enough extinction.

Near six, seabirds laugh, the bells
shout out for worshipers to pray.

Star Matter at Work

A man came to my door
saying that he, like I, had questioned
unsaintly scientists' good faith, i.e.
bona fides. He proffered to me
science as corrugation, obfuscation,
bent imagination, curving space, "realities"
much too recondite that I might pinpoint
unquestioned azimuths of authority
for any path through human space.

"Why choose me?" "Out of the blue."
"Why tell me of things I cannot know?"
"Hey, doesn't Goldman, Sachs do the same?"
"Won't I bump into my steel table
when I know the atomic configuration?"
"Get used to ephemeral realities, hug no box
but scientific thought outside the box:
we are the "stuff" of stars; repeat
we are the "stuff" of stars.

Since that day, probably coincidently,
notice has appeared in selective media
confirming allegations in obscure works
that we are star matter standing to order
for new purposes and unlimited progeny.

Although long-gone, the man imbues me.
Excitedly I marry all debarking visitors
(Embarrassed, I conceal involuntary erections),

I want for nothing, but hope for everything,
including progressive taxes by the legislature.

My neighbors seem troubled by star matter
as it compromises community rules and by
my space rigid in salute of scientific discovery.

Government Man

Having come more than 2000 miles in summer heat,
the government man enters the arena cross; he knows
that people here hold a grudge, for 80 years, since FDR;

he will deal with the New Deal later. Now, he explains
that Plan A, diplomacy, is always the preferred strategy;
that a full invasion, Plan B, will apply only if the powerless
can persuade the powerful too. Civil butchery continues.

The man explains: "Expect a brief occupation, during which
sectarian hostilities likely will re-emerge; it's generational:
slaughter arises as second nature." He asks the world press
to swell fervency until we guide them to the promised-land.

Further, the man alludes to inscrutability, like mothers' milk;
its implacability, so we too must prepare implacably to kill
with redundant force if necessary. Please support our shame.

The government man reminds all citizens, even if reluctant,
to empathize, to send humanitarian aid promptly as death
persists disproportionately to national self-interests; that
prompt contributions now benefit the world's economy.

Tests to fill a shortage of government men are given daily.
In time more government men will come to explain FDR.

One Cat of Many

This cat claimed Angst as his name early, covered in wolfish fur from which yellow eyes erupted not in Sinai fire but old man lethargy. A kitten fiercely burdened with a legacy of Moses, not committed to God's will, but the final Jew for travail of miles just now clear of Egypt. His ambience saturated me, because of course intelligence fitted keenly to language cannot be his forte, so we have gone along a good part of a cat's expected existence, revealing very little of our separate essences, me at my books, he privately ineluctable.

Las Vegas, Refuge for a Christian Nation

Christians alone in the universe
straining first to reach,
then on the long ride home,
to cleanse their sins.

Conscience makes a hard bargain:
what happens in Las Vegas
stays in Las Vegas.

Impending Weather

A man came to my door
warning that low barometric pressure
would approach from the sea,
followed by torrential rains
guided by the hand of God.

I knew of this impending weather,
although Channel 4's report
apparently lacked important details.

I had dug many curtain drains,
knowing the gravity of flood waters.

I had hauled tons of river rock
to stave off potential ruin.

But I had not known that
I would be subject to God's wrath
or that Channel 4 would abuse
my trust that it serve the public
at its frequency on the air waves.

Pride of Lions

Smudge's classic cat face evolved a dark spot along his jaw. No mirror
was ever provided him, but his singular talent as a mark of his distinction
enlarged his personality every day: soon he was beautiful; around a central
oracle a community of three, Smudge and Angst opposing males, and Vixen
the feminine transfixing their attention at the rustling of surround-
ing leaves.

In my time, in my world, such presences typically abash, their
source of pride.

Rust Honors a Bloom

Cool water would hit the spot, yet, abandoned,
a water tower rusts above a desert highway.

Further, a settler misplaced trust in a friend
for a quit claim shack. History marks the event
with a sign among rattlers facing their survival.

I have water handy. I refresh. I check the tower
for lessons: always leave footprints in the dust,
burnishings and sweat. Dehydration threatens,
paint wears and chips in wind from inside out,
wind whipped in Death Valley to wreak its worse.

An unknown flower blooms, enough to turn me round
and linger, to sniff its scent, oxidized, greased and oiled.

A fuel stop welcomes me to rapidly diminishing supply.

Malice

A man came to my door
to say directly to my face that I
had chosen him alone to malign
in places he was still known, often
where he had established good will.

He wore prominently a patriarchal cross,
like a sword, apparently very weighty,
and when he worshiped, my atheism
insinuated an added burden. He shopped
as if lost among goods in the shopping center:
my new tire preference made his own car
ride noisily and roughly, even on macadam.
Certain in-laws, trusting his wife's liberalism,
and aware of his aversion to me, questioned
his judgment and her tolerance of it.
Almost all New England was now polluted.

He could kill me at my door.
(As yet I saw no weapon.) I said "Hold on!"

That I used an exclamation point, apparently
armed with grammar was finally too much.

For discerning readers of poetry
I don't need to say
what happened after that.

Photo Dreams at Thanksgiving

I hadn't figured time rightly.
A minute gone may be a year.

Then Fall photos flitted by
on my computer, like movies
in the theater of my past;
recast my eye at red, orange
colors; ghostly shaped spells;
fresh, audacious, bold acuity:
light of photographers' dreams.

Time, so it happens, diffuses
like rain filtering through silt;
often inconsequential forever
or until the future moment
casts its light, such as morning.

I got the mood right, but mood
blackens, must ask forgiveness.

Don't revisit those goblins alone.
Holiday good gets much better.
Take children. Build traditions
of tricks, treats and time passing.

Voices in the Belfry

I met for years with contrary shades
of my own being, pressed heatedly my claims;
duly performed suitable penalties;
hauled from life's mine tons of ore.

In fact, some arguments rang with truth,
bestowed its honor on me from both my sides;
however, most floundered in superstition.

Sometimes eloquent, I presented my pains
and my glimmerings in artificial light,
on which everyone I knew depended too.

None may speak for pains unfelt.
The scar is authority for the lash.
Piled dross recites the purity of gold.
Shaky drafts embed worth in the final poem.

I have a small hill.
I like traveling long roads.
I have an ear for immaculate tone.
But I have forged no golden bell,
still work in congress to make a belfry.

Unwelcome with My Camera?

Local folks suspect strangers lurking about.
My head up, I gauge light burst on a window,
then as flashily decamps in the leaves' flutter.
What to do with "get away from my lawn"?
Or defend a case of brilliance here observed?

If I turn to gaze farther I dig ghastly cavities
in brain matter granted custody of this place.

All right, a simple inquiry at the door: May I
pause to limn the gilding pageantry of light?
Thus squandering that time and all should he
answer "NO!" East breeze ferries drama in;
rain sweeps to vertical the velour of leaves;
street spray from a car flashes the horizontal.

A tide no more regularly reconfigures beach
than light saturates this neighborhood's eyes
blinding in painted white of this church wall
of a minor sect sparkling as if combustible.

My accidental presence here creates a scene:
a timeless day, my imperfect finger ready on
the release; my ignorance; me, wet but steadily
pelted by as yet unknown but eternal certainties.

A forced departure bars me from final assertion,
penultimate views, or any of infinite assertions
on any stage where my vision may earn a space.

Evening darkness, of course, supplants debate,
yet a word: I click a frame to the mediating, but
minor sect, yet in profile. Kinfolk tales portend
a fight, but guide the fine spirit of nostalgic light.

Reading at Park Place Books

Thanks for coming. I like intimate gatherings.

I wrote my new poem to read aloud to friends,
but also to anonymous listeners to be thrilled.

I bet myself (a stinging wager for either side)
that reading aloud confronts an animal fear,
like a rat gnawing at my ulna, at my knee,
at my toes in the dark before sleep;
that I confront strangers aware of my
singularity (like a black hole?), courageous
among my demons from my dark forest
to speak reminiscences in dusky cadences,
to be greeted heartily by dutiful word-fellows,
all haughty heroes laden with leaf wreathes
and hurrahs that will echo through history.

And so I do this thing.
I come with felicitous words.
Such is my gift.

Walking Stick, A Prayer

At hand, my sturdy oak rod, truly saved itself
by lightning, suffices as listener to my ambling
prayers. The spreading sky and following road
become my tabernacle, a peregrine my deacon.
My family at the farm engage in life well-bred,
raised with devotion to the spirit we are born
to tend; that duty is well-begun; for her duty,
mother was well-anointed as our shepherdess.
Attend me closely as I walk mother, guide me
from nether bramble into my salvation. Amen.

Rebellion Takes up Conspiracy with Mankind

Howard Thomas had grown engagingly human.
He nurtured Harry S. Truman, his heretical cat.
Howard, who had many, often invited
friends to visit him for bracing conversation
about what it meant to be engagingly human.

Howard provoked his friends to act feline;
occasionally, his friends engaged with claws.
More than ten feline friends are hard to herd.
But Howard rationalized that his humanity
could resist even the bloodshed of rebellion,
that as long as his friends stayed in his parlor
and did not spread their cat insurrection outside
the rest of Mankind would embrace their differences.

Harry S. knew better. Harry S. would have preferred
that *his instincts* led the cat skirmish, from atop a cabinet,
a favorite place. Harry S. Truman got exact terms
he wanted when human rebellion
took up conspiracy with Mankind.

Afterwards, Howard came to believe
that humanity will not be engaged
nor be well served by soothing purrs.

As a hermit, Howard expanded
the biography of notable cats.
Harry S sought other comforts.

Tending Roses, an Observance

(for Sylvia)

Essential pragmatism in your garden
ignores blight, the broken limb; plows
your determination through stems
and petals, all supporting your light.

Light, rain spark life's spiky rejoinders.
Each rose evinces your sound science.

You animate neighbors' to titillation,
who turned heads to Madame Alfred
Carriere, an antique queen, and Just Joey,
a rascal always pricking a passing skirt:
rank immodesty compels the olfactory.

Through aphid blights, mildew, black
spot, and toll of all—personal failure—
should life in a doomed bud drain away
in the back acre, you tend to roots (I'll
call it spirit), and let blooms be blooms.

In the garden, many know of dormancy.
Most think death. Few note the future.
You sense tincture rising in the stalk;
aroma pervasive through duress; and
shivers of silk opening bravely in sun.
If only truth in politics was as clear.

May I hallow your observant loyalty
and attend you as a neophyte might?
I will learn the way. I lean idealistic,
true, hoping that disease is only spite.

Prerogatives

I am sorry to tell you
that of all men here
you are least privileged.

This is a practical result
of all men being equal.
Of course, you ask why?

You ask if this is my joke.
I assure you this is history.

No sir, resolution is not near.

I do not presume revolution.

Well, I write poetry. Privileged?
Not in the way you may assume
and perhaps even less than you.

Yes, I have studied our history.
Yes, there is an ugly consistency.
Yes, do not look beyond greed,
nor hatred of our fellow equals.

No, there is no logic to hatred.
No, greed is apparently unbounded.
No, for some there is no restraint
on freedom; government is feckless.

Therefore, those who believe
that superiority ought to rule,
are privileged to assert prerogative.

Later Life: Think Harder, but Remain Silent

Go Somewhere without Saying

I hoped to deflect an impertinent remark.

The best rebuttal I thought of on the spot,
a thing clever, yet decisive? *Forensic fact*
admissible in court wraps us totally now,
hooks our noses toward unsavory sniffs.

And so I temporarily diverted the probe.
Of course at issue was defense of poetry.
Indefensible, I often hear it proclaimed.

My work suffuses modern or recent history,
but at only 71 my knowledge may be slight:
finer points of understanding passed away
with compromise, so decisive cleverness
presupposes spin with foxes in their dens.

I heard a poet proudly riddle about a truth,
critical inexactitude, with fiendish pride:
I asked him, remembering a phase, would
he repudiate anarchy? He doubted my call.

Then I doubted my call, retreated to details
of fundamental earthiness, play in the dirt;
play in snow; play in a stream sans salmon;
play in surf fearing undertow. What more?

Then I coined the word associational poem.
Facing that question, I shook another week
before regaining courage to challenge words.

To the initiated, all this goes without saying,
so with the rest of my poem I seek initiation.

The pearl sits in dew on a lotus blossom.
The chief eunuch stands guard over a harem.
Which, at that place, would go without saying.

Ideas Relegated

News finally came down. More
had occurred than I had thought.

Earth's mis-alignment punished
some unfortunates for positions
occupied since ancient times, but
growing less hospitable whether
direct or indirect in the sun's rays.

Others banish to lesser regions all
unable to escape centrifugal weight
as lower rungs of human hierarchy,
not to raise up, nor fortify, nor care.

The waters rise, of course, torrents
flow from melt on high, threatening
flood once more, destructive ideas
too relegated, but in much argument.

An Act of Conscience

My code ensures your security.
My intellect dominates me, so
no army needs to offer its help.

But inside I conceal a predator
heart that tempts to track game
afoot until my predator heart
apprehends my prey's heart
a brief instant before a kill.

A trophy waits in my aim;

my mind releases the hammer.

Possible Parallels

A single hiker on the road, not obviously obsessive,
plods forward. The more remote the road, the more
he plods forward, the more the single mind obsesses.

He may prefer daylight, but, to reach an end planned
for this day, yields to a few more miles into darkness.
He knows that dying light has long sped ahead of him,
and, continuing, he gains on morning, more obsession.

Another hiker, amid general population, gets distracted:
traffic lights burst in the foreground; peripheral sparking
lays on the finite optic nerve; sight diminishes at night.
This road is similarly built, lain for commercial cartage
rather than astral siege; lain to deny pleasing wanderers;
lain in uncouth macadam above which no dream unfolds.

Every road affords a truth to a hiker. But truth springs
from wind, rises from night, changes by photosynthesis,
bends space, breeds a lily, emits a light, yet emerges in
waste, collects as residue, drifts as dust, piles as grit on
the ashen plain as the day's ache writhes into muscles.

X   X   X   X

The physicist drove a manageable distance on a chosen
road, did not stop to conceive quantum, the impossible
parallel motoring beside what had always been probable.

I stop myself in shared, ordinary, linear time. I proceed
again without Einstein relativities, without special focus,
rather the blur of zipping lights costing great effort to see
new shapes: my mathematics works when it makes sense.

Thoroughbreds Race, an Allegorical Polemic

Each horse a champion, prancing its bloodline pride:
nurtured on oats, brushed coats, glossed and bronzy,
blazoned by silks to the finish, aristocrats of charm.

But a stallion, Swift Corruption, commands the track;
baffles the underdogs, especially Reform, a gelding,
first forcing it to the rail, then crowding it at the turn.
The muddy track with a good bottom favors a devil
in a deep blue sea, another bounty for corrupt repute:
a hose pours puddles in the infield, at the quarter pole.

But greed cheers Corruption; its mechanical motion;
its manes unstrained; its slight ankles pumping pistons
that bet life on a win; its royal progress at the final turn;
its trod of losers down the straightaway spotted in dirt.

Reform carries its colors to place, no threat to the lead.
Reform can but sniff Corruption's tail, braided with silk.

A few self-restrained fans may praise the haughty beast.
Even my lazy, incorruptible eye notes a rippling energy;
its easy gait exploding to a race; the spell to seduce our
repeated presence; its command rivets us at full attention;
its wild breath; its obliging wreath of magnificent flowers.

In the circle, Corruption nuzzles a bulging purse, lighted
eyes shine like the sun. Yet, time guarantees no favors,
nor promises additional starts. To make its bed of roses,
a winner must grease many palms. Comely mares sidle
by, slim, sleek, and eager in display to new generations.

Milton Friedman Revels

Mechanize economics to regurgitate profit

Compound echelon-earned interest

Privatize the zoo and each little zoolet

Miss Plutocrat presents her roseate cheek
*   *   *

Wall Street shines in spite of oxygen-deficiency
*   *   *

The stench we all breathe is called neoliberalism.
*   *   *

Milton, your God takes notice and will be impressed
*   *   *

People are granted baby licenses, home licenses,
cow licenses if they can persuade the cows to come home
to swell the crowd watching the boot-strapping spectacle.

Resistance

My forearm strains at a root.
Perhaps in fine soil, I pushed
my trowel too aggressively.

In the garden I am pretender
at best, rigged with intentions
to meet the Master's needs.

Now, desperation builds apace.
Important assumptions fail me.
Resistance makes me impotent.

A Chip on My Shoulder

No, I don't have what the title up there says;
no blind tumult in my synapses, if indeed I
continue a belief in synapses; no motive to
carry on belief in slivers of wood or stone,
small, typically flat, useless and disregarded;
nor today forever present integrated circuits,
icons that last an hour, unlike a chiseled rune.

I do, in actual fact, reject easy reality, favoring
rather the diamond "hard," unreduced essences
of the Precambrian, not expecting the "rough."

Such my preamble to my place in space, lodged
between celestial zenith and nadir, amid my devils.

Options

Time, like a reservoir, can fill. In drought
we spot those tree stumps so easy to forget.

Passing, most of my pond of time emptied,
then lapsed perpetually. Events that seemed
important, maybe for intricacy, bold color,
coarse texture, scent evocative, volatile,
lingered in my nose, displaced by offal.

Even once important friends who pledged
to play the measure with me, to avail me
for distances before diverging, retreated
where I could never settle but they felt
compelled. How does one choice stick?
How does the blue comber thrust? How
does pink granite rasp? How hear poetry
of the discharging ovum? As life abides,
more time freely abdicates, less freely
fits my barrel of rifle bore precision.

I must fix on one urge at a time, permit
pot shops at speculation: a tugboat bobs
up more than forward, its dance above
the bay's ripple, its plod to inevitability,
oil spit in smoke, its yield to loosening
muster of rivets and welds wildly romantic.

Green, then golden wheat on the Palouse,
as light agitates above, energizing a hill

and field to shanghai every breeze, force
each to circle and flutter the flag leaves;
and there, the fetching female's bird walk,
spin, exaggerating her sex for an old man.

This last is no option, merely an enticing
confection that bakers keep on baking up.

Nearby, but Incognito

Crows could blacken the sky with wings
without any two colluding or in concert.
Two crows might sit closely on a wire,
face opposite ways to see the same future.

Think of me as nearby, but incognito.
I can know so little of your life, always
wanting to know more. Like a dog's tail
wagging excitedly, impossible to still,
eager to ingratiate with human company.

Years ago we discussed friendship, loyalty
and respect. These principles, however,
can weaken in time, expanding distance
intervening. A western storm may arrive,
typically, but the favorite elm has fallen
and the pet collie has been killed, both
occupants of our local sacred spaces.
Marauding crows sit on branches and
know in collective darkness the difference.

Your rock-solid mother, always kind to me
and more, an advocate, a friend; she passed
leaving craters across our landscape. Do you
see me now, by the stream, stamping dust
in frustration, beneath the remaining oak?

Diplomacy's Obligation to History

Each word, each act, each memory requires recording
at the instant spoken, acted or remembered, including
tone of voice, contextualization of events, and editorial
asides deemed worthy of remark to spur history's dialog.
Details from savvy observers can strangle propaganda:
peculiar conditions cited best prove the memory true.

Reports sent home must survive authority's rigorous sift;
"shock" and "dismay" tighten tongues of those entitled
to access; the streets of capitals flutter with dead leaves
that after cordoning will advise the press and populate
the manuscripts elucidating compromise. Built on lies?
Realpolitik? Or pusillanimous pretenders to leadership?

Latest Life, Shout Out Loud

In Memory of Ken Patterson

At its beginning forty years ago, this poem was formless and void.
I don't remember precisely a sequence of first days and nights,
but with Ken there was energy of new light, separate from the dark,
big concepts unfolding, San Francisco streets, horns and screen doors,
babysitting his niece and honey Ianthe whose affinity was mud butt.

Time on the surface of the deep gets fuzzed up: we recall cool fogs,
but not actual street integers, not pastel Frisco pastiches, nor any one
of the Giants except Chris Speier at short, so soon after Willie Mays;
Watergate, but I'm sure neither Ken nor God had hHis hand in that;
caftans and bare feet, for which both Ken and Charlotte were at fault.

Ken thought in galactic terms, faced the meteors, unlike my terror
to face a trillion stars: I shudder even now to reason how beginnings,
whether voids or bangs can be unappreciated, perhaps left in the trunk
of an old car, the subjects of postal errors, or now undeliverable email
destined as dysfunction for the great recycle bin trailing the asteroid belt.

The old times were real. Ken needed them defined: notes, his symbols,
drawings of the space arc, mapped coordinates with the largest views,
left turns and right turns for the smaller view, to head into then return
from unusual or crooked avenues, dead end streets and parks of
free air.

Golden Gate and the Planetarium, centers of Ken's universe, *omphalos*
for the old Greeks, grassy and rhododendry for me basking in sunshine
cooled by ocean breezes while Ianthe rode to freedom on a statue
of a horse.

These are credible foundations for lasting duration, not requiring mortar,
rebar, special license, nor education, nor bribes of city officials and cronies.
Ken, Charlotte, Sylvia, Ianthe and I came west out of pure luck: I scoured
plains for wagon tracks, Ken took Venus from Orion's belt to etch a memory.

Curious Oddities

Wholly black night repellent to stars,
but wide open to a holy pale moon
hovering through an arc, but nightly,
in emptiness. What is this to my place?

My terror at stars without end dissipates;
stages of ghost moons reform, then others.

What energy remains to me still pulls me;
I cannot pause, knowing what I now know.

Now aged 73
I know I will die
if my curiosity
about heavenly
freak shows
fritters out.

Ascent without Firm Link

Memories must be banned from exactitude.
Things of today spark me alive, of course.
But if today reminds me of yesterday, then
it merely jars me to doubt what can happen
tomorrow? Yesterday comes as a phantom;
merges like primary red and blue as purple;
plunges like water over the lip of the falls,
impossible to re-frame the river's argument;
feelings of the flesh that are only forgettings,
not real events. Memories smother like fog,
unnerving each step that guides me to a peak.

Missed Opportunity over Coffee

Our meeting was a fluke, no premeditation at all,
one in a thousand with a dropped cap introduction.

And such a coincidence: we both had developed
a taste for coffee, cream but no sugar: a fortunate
beginning. I thought to know you. As a friend?

The misunderstanding was entirely on my side.

Prepared to discuss other mutual interests, I did
not ask about your politics. When they emerged,
not immediately, but buds of innuendo, shorthand
opinions, confusing allusions to media thinkers,
praises for the rule of law, particularly punitive.

I recoiled. I stood. I apologized; I had to leave.
You called me "doctrinaire." To support this,
you cited as source undisputed alternative facts.

Even Later, Dribble and Spit

Venom, Virtue and Fun

**"Only a virtuous people are capable of freedom.
As nations become more corrupt and vicious, they
have more need of masters." Benjamin Franklin**

Some among us risk the edge of reason;
some dispute fealty to constitutional oaths;
some laugh at, some fear others' ideologies;
some may lord over us with wit and whip:

such a one as the unrepentant queen of venom,
whose virtue, yet, is not questioned: Ann Coulter.

That I suffer my affinities dark too, like coffee;
that purpose in a cause can be a special blend;
that my reliance on cream prompts Ann's sugar.

But my refreshment is no act to incite, naught
but synaptic charge through dark energy that,
with Ann, boils off for a thick, true espresso; we
both evidence deep distrust of our human nature,
an encomium beneath water of a polluted pool
in which we drown if we choose not to swim.

Ann lifts her cup in praise of the pointedly pure.

The Cratered Road to Malancourt: Doughboys Face the Meuse-Argonne

Our general plows the muddy clay, then coughs:
"Gentlemen, I approve the corps, division and
regimental battle plans, without amendment."

Craters before Malancourt lie equaled beyond,
a formation of deadly mathematical precedent.

Green officers and men engage each landscape
not so much as luxuries of lush green space, but
blasted, burned lairs to fears and secreted enemies.

Friendly artillery cracks a redoubt, sunders a wall,
exposes tender viscera, the array of enemy troops,
or rents bodies to sift like powder per the mission.

When "heavies" form craters, soldiers vaporize,
unable to sidestep the rapid concert, demolition
little described in *The Science of Artillery* texts.

"Where be the heart of the matter? How dwells
the angel of mercy in such screams from hell?
What point reveals life not lost but liquefied?"

Reconstruction, a Conversation

Yes, slavery days discharged the stink of black sweat,
life on the block, available to my touch before buying.

And such delightful entertainment, fruit of prerogative.
I tingle at the thought, whether female or male. Surely
we had dollars at stake and depletion by inordinate heat.

I'm no historian, we lose truth's angle, how heartstrings
quaver as our comforts, even reputation, may be ruined.
Also, the war. Your name cropped up at cards last night.

Ode to Mitch

Smells shuffle noxiously, not fusty
or rancid like local organics afloat
over the paper manufacturing plant,
but some process foreign, imported
stink from our native robber baron
returned now, to invest in our town
and vault America to new greatness.

Crowds assemble to attend the man,
greet him with nosegays swaddling
their noses, cackles convulsing their
voices, withering throats of gratitude.

Hold! He speaks: "Fellow citizens,
ladies and gentlemen, Republicans,
let us pray for our glorious leader
who has taught us as Americans how
we should act in our communities and
in the world! God bless Mr. Trump!"

"Mitch, what is that disgusting smell?"

Expected Disappearance

Still young, I learned that postures tended
to come with inheritance, to dominate sway
in my neighborhood, as unstated traditions.

Generations would gather as if in a church,
nonsectarian, from St. Louis and its environs
assured that their own and prior family souls
would guide our childhoods toward modesty.

My dad wore dungarees, as did we three sons;
kept us out of poverty; no dark suit, no fedora;
pushed a bladed mower across our spiky grass
we charitably (with minor posture) called "lawn."

Never in a holy sanctuary, I promised some deity
(purely intuited without a formal metaphysics),
but usual to my home at the Gateway to the West
to make my first Atlantic Ocean trip adventurous
rather than reverent, fun with no duty. But waves
buffeted me, their constancy expected, but not
my weak obedience to a dominant, unknown sea,
their utter power hurtling a shark, dead yes, but
not a lifeless corpse, rolled at me teeth first still
intent to consume humanity by starting with me,
ripping my gushing flesh, to bleed me pure white.

These memories displaced posture. No longer 20,
no longer 70, I prefer a peaceful demise, perhaps
without chartreuse liqueur and flowers, but frisky

kittens rolling across my fingers and nibbling my
cold hands, my casket dignified by carpenter's eye.

Perhaps friends would surround me, likely to enjoy
the late summer sun rays as, ostensibly, I disappear.

Ever Improving

My fondness is not hard to express
here at the waterfront. I come often,
my eyes tearing in combined currents,
purposing a benign, mystic flagellation.

I walk nearby new aluminum turbines
rotating in wind, producing no power.
I approach the old fishing pier and see
cottonwood stumps from earlier time,
cut and milled to restrain fishers past.
The old pier warps in ways weird for
wood, and sits in a decrepit condition.
The new city pier may be used, strong,
sunk deep in the shoreline by the creek,
"improved" per city elders (not fishers),
being pestered by boat and public traffic.

I especially note the galvanized chains
looped around the edges of the pier and
carrying a motif to the sculpted octopus,
freed from ubiquitous rust from salt air.

Now that almost all the fish are gone,
now that fisher numbers have reduced,
tide waters roil, new barnacles grasp,
the breezes hoist on me a sting of loss.

Early Workday at the Marina

The tug engine purrs with confidence within hearing
of an unknown number of marina tenants; echoes
a clarion to begin the workday. In stages, vessels stir
at the sound of alert, their captains filled with purpose,
but without panic. These men condition themselves
to moods of nature, ready at release of mooring ropes
to challenge their insecurity at the changing unknown.
I see their dignity, assurance, sensing the humidity,
temperature, mountain and oceanic mood, all effect
on life aboard. The tug's purr offered good harbinger:
pier traffic increases beneath a sky sullen as late-night
radio without advantage of enlivening by local guests.

Doubloon

The shore whets a boy's longing for adventure.
He jitterbugs on smooth stones burning his soles.
On the horizon, a sailboat hauls anchor, pinning
his psyche, visible to all, like a doubloon nailed
by Ahab to the mast.
"Spy me that whale, my boy.
Sing me a whale song. Sing me a white whale song!"
And the shanty rings with tones of gold singing.

Aligned with other whaling men, the boy hauls
the hawser aboard, his fantasy to follow the dive,
through spume, into the dark, though told not to.

Patience and Urgency

A sandy stretch where no wave has borne in for a while.
The fisher who could have been on the sea but got old.
A necessary dose of reason held, which he had supplied.

And still everything thought, most things known, failed.

The sculptor toiled, often almost falling into the brazier;
he who would hesitate may have won, but in a lesser way;
such raw value suffused in the shape need not be annealed.

And still failures mounted. The heron stepped. And fished
where it sometimes knew success, but certainly not always.

Forged, a mask hides identity, finally to distort the message.

Fish deplete, for which the fisher, insensate, cannot mourn.

Olympic Discovery Trail Monday Questions

Forest Disciple Stripped

A red cedar log has been abandoned
to currents of the Salish Sea, drifted
to this sheltered bay, to lie stranded
on basalt rocks lining the pedestrian
shore, finally lodged, come to rest.

Who will repudiate its ragged scars,
its unquiet felling, peeling red bark?

Where did it fall? Clear cuts abound
on the nutcracker's heights. Would a
nutcracker refuse a proffered peanut?;
abet a logger with another scalping?;
accompany a tree to its deep descent?;
mount a resistance on a tree's behalf?;
denude a tree's protective bark; delimb,
stress a bole to split and crack, dump
an icon of romance to float and bob?

This castaway proves unwelcome to
denizens of the Salish Sea; it pricks
the herons, the ubiquitous gulls, and
raccoons shuffling by as if a squatter,
tongue lolling, indifferent to its death.

The Beak Penetrates

A crow drops its prey from its beak,
plummets to retrieve it on the shell,
guts the bivalve like a true gourmand.

A satisfactory meal of clam depends
on a durable shell and adductor hinge.

I'm here mainly for exercise, after which
I'll return to sup with the crow on the pier.Olympic Discovery
Olympic Discovery Trail Monday Questions

Midwesterner as Tourist

My place presents forever flat vistas
seeking horizons in every direction,
seething displacement without calm.

This place is much different, as I see.
Will you tell me how to stand erect
when only the bay surface is level?

Of course you may refuse to answer.
Will I offend if I ask your reasoning?
Would you agree that these differences
will tend to provoke bitterness except
when the clouds settle on our heads?
Do we dare to believe our ideas false?

Do you also tend to avoid your time?

Drops of Water in the World;
Worlds in a Drop of Water

A pleasure craft departs the marina.

It crosses the bay leisurely. Its captain
appears to pursue a destined heaven,
which may be only the bobbing bay,
breeze in his face, the ease of an open
lane (cargo ships wait to load or unload),
relish enough to overlap each moment.

Ancient minds conjectured heavens, left
elliptical images on walls, animal gods,
or writings on vellum or papyrus; over
glaze of pottery, in the teardrops of gold,
or salt tears pursuing wistful salvation;
in the certain expostulations of priests;
in denigrations of the occupants of Hell.

Waves splinter to drops before the boat,
splash atop the deck, drench his cheek:
drops of water in the captain's world;
worlds embraced in a drop of water.

Today at the Pier

Much circus-like frenzy fills the street, pier
and ferry parking holding area, livening air.

Tourists watch the captain position his ship,
with engines in reverse, at the dock, roped,
and aligned for aft debarkation from Victoria.

I wanted eyes to flame out at the maneuver,
as mine so often have: I time the event daily.
Skills of this kind, at this level, beg attention.
Yet all who watched the big ship enter the bay
have moved on, from thirty or more to but one.

Would the namesake, the plump Coho Salmon,
bob in shallows and escape public intrusion?
Fathers with notoriously coy daughters, desert
the pier, not caring to share a pleasure with me.

Shorebirds off the Salish Sea

The great blue goes bronze in wait
of prey, so erect as wind tickles surf;
the gull flies past, too impatient;
the heron moves to attend an object
beneath the water's surface; the gull
flies past.

The earthworm hugs
the trail in the same direction
at the same deliberate heron speed:

the sunset transforms a bird to art.

Tourists' Pleasure

Competing birds began hungry, now become belligerent
as they circle my head. Hearing ageless animal dispute
sets my imagination a-wing, to seek any grubs or seeds,
or the garbage of tourists pleasure-seeking on the beach.

I Pause at the Lake to Wait for You

Life, even his life, does not touch my friend.

If this is fact, can it be so simple?
To go from one place to another?
To act one part after another?

In time the road is revised;
the modus alters; by a lake
the shoreline shifts; maps
lag behind and must catch up;
the seasons always change.

Life as I know it
does not touch my friend.
Simplicity never touches my friend.

After bad seasonal starts,
I pursue the unchanged.
Recently I found this in your love.

Five in a Day

The wash
adores the bow's design.

Water, by bobbing cupful,
abets the breeze.

The distant craft
gambols in swells.

Seabirds
reconvene darkly at the dock.

Day hastens
west of the sea's defeat into dark.

2 Bison Confer on Past and Future Wanderings

(a dialog occurring outside others' hearing)

B1: "I've been in the area a long time and cannot recall our ever meeting."

B2: "I expect that is the case, because our territories are vast. Our groups are so much smaller, I cannot call them 'herds', but still so few of us have truly distinctive features."

B1: "Certainly! How has 'bison life' been for you?"

B2: "Mostly it's dull going and hot, or dull going and freezing cold. But I do get chased and nipped by the occasional wolf, or must wade through hip high snow for a bit of grass without any nutritional value at all; scrub and sage mostly, dust and dearth."

B1: "You've got terrific linguistic rhythm for such a ponderous beast! How did you learn?"

B2: "Overhearing tourists while I laze chewing my cud."

B1: "I can't claim anything as exciting as that! Do you have adventures you would be willing to share?"

B2: "Well, I need to be going soon, but thanks for asking. I do have one that cracks me up every time I recall it. I was out for pleasure, wallowing in one of the large, arid parks when around a bend comes this Volkswagen Beetle, yellow, man and woman. One step and I was in the center of the road, standing taller than the car. It was near dusk. The cows and calves were safely away. You can imagine the looks on their faces: near closing of the park; 3 miles to the west exit, 50 miles to the east exit, maybe a fine if they fail to vacate!"

B1:   "What did you do?"

B2:   "Nothun'! I stood firm, 2000 pounds of road block! It tickled me to death!"

B1:   "Well?"

B2:   "After a few minutes of joy, I started walking straight at the snub nose of that little Beetle. Back he whined (you know how they do) in reverse. On I clopped on the black top road. Back he whined! Another brand of unexpected hilarity!"

B1:   "I'm so envious I could pee! So you just walked right over that hood in the front, right?"

B2:   "No, sorry, but I felt no malice for the poor folks, just my way of partying. Finally, I just wandered off into the brush and let them be on their way."

B2:   "Well, this has been good, but there's boredom to explore. Maybe we'll tangle horns again someday. Nice meeting you B1."